Retold and Illustrated by the Children and
Teachers of Ibapah Elementary School

Pia Toya
A Goshute Indian Legend

The University of Utah Press
Salt Lake City

Proceeds from the sale of this book benefit a cultural education foundation established in the name of the Confederated Tribes of the Goshute.

LIBRARY OF CONGRESS CATALOGING-IN-PUBLICATION DATA

Pia Toya : A Goshute Indian legend / retold and illustrated by the children and teachers of Ibapah Elementary.
   p. cm.
Summary : Retells the story of the creation of the Deep Creek Mountains by Mother Hawk after Coyote steals her breakfast.
Includes information on the Goshute people, legends, and history.

   ISBN 0-87480-661-5
 1. Gosiute Indians—Folklore. 2. Legends—Great Basin. 3. Creation—Mythology. [1. Gosiute Indians—Folklore. 2. Indians of North America—Great Basin—Folklore. 3. Folklore—Great Basin. 4. Creation—Folklore.] I. Ibapah Elementary School (Ibapah, Utah)
   E99.G67 P53 2000
   398.2'089'97—dc21

00-008822

06   05   04   03   02   01   00

5   4   3   2   1

In the time before the people,

the land we know as Ibapah Valley
was a large mountain region.

Tamara Zollinger

Isapai-ppeh, the coyote, lived there on one lonely mountain.

Marcie Thomas

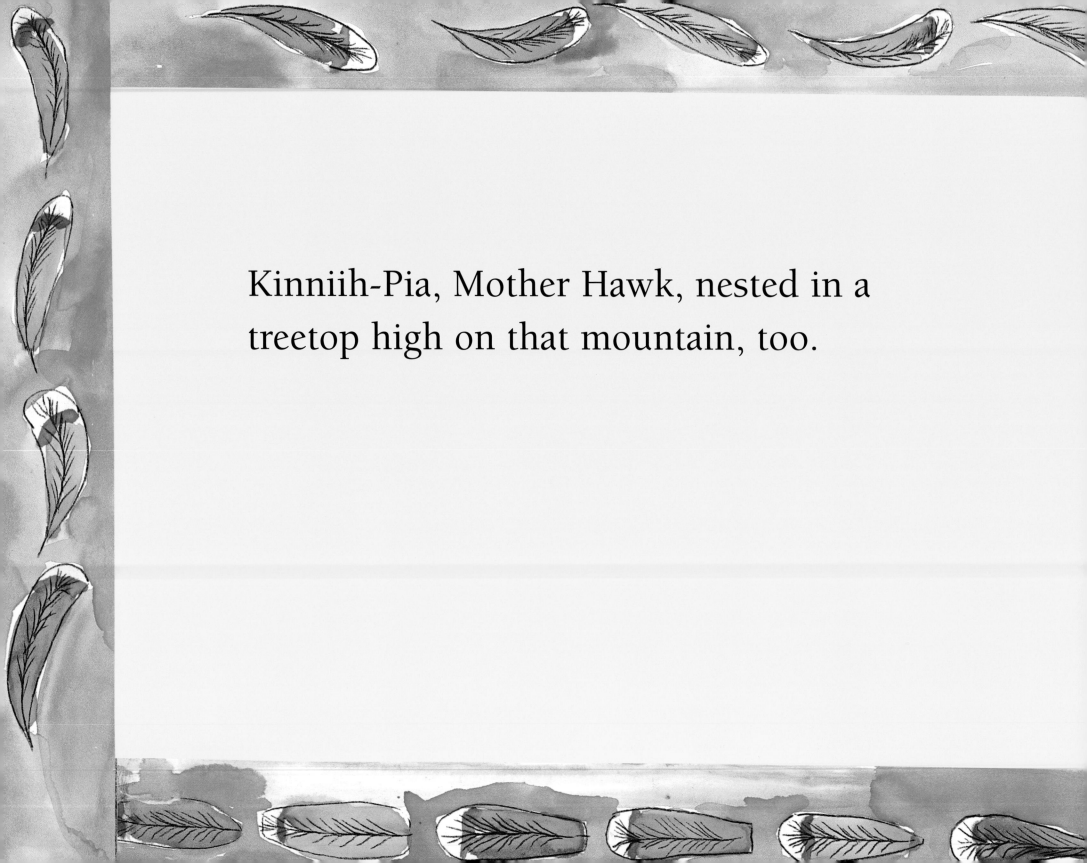

Kinniih-Pia, Mother Hawk, nested in a treetop high on that mountain, too.

Early one morning Mother Hawk flew to the ground. She held her breakfast in her claws, a small gray mouse.

Coyote knew of Mother Hawk's breakfast. He had seen her capture it. Coyote was hungry, too, so he sneaked up behind Mother Hawk. As he came close he thought up a plan to make Mother Hawk's breakfast his own.

Mr. John Thomas

"Mother Hawk," Coyote said, "you are so mighty and powerful. Look through the trees. Do you see the fat rabbit hopping there? He would make a fine breakfast for you."

Ed Lorenzo

Mother Hawk looked up from the mouse for just a moment. Quick as lightning Coyote snatched it from her.

Tamara Zollinger

"Give back the breakfast you have stolen from me," Mother Hawk said. Her voice seemed to shake the air with its power.

"And what will you do if I do not?" asked Coyote. Before she could answer, Coyote swallowed the mouse in one quick gulp.

Tamara Zollinger

Mother Hawk became angry. She pounded her wings and flew up into the sky. She watched Coyote and then, without warning, swooped down on him.

Nathan
Hicks

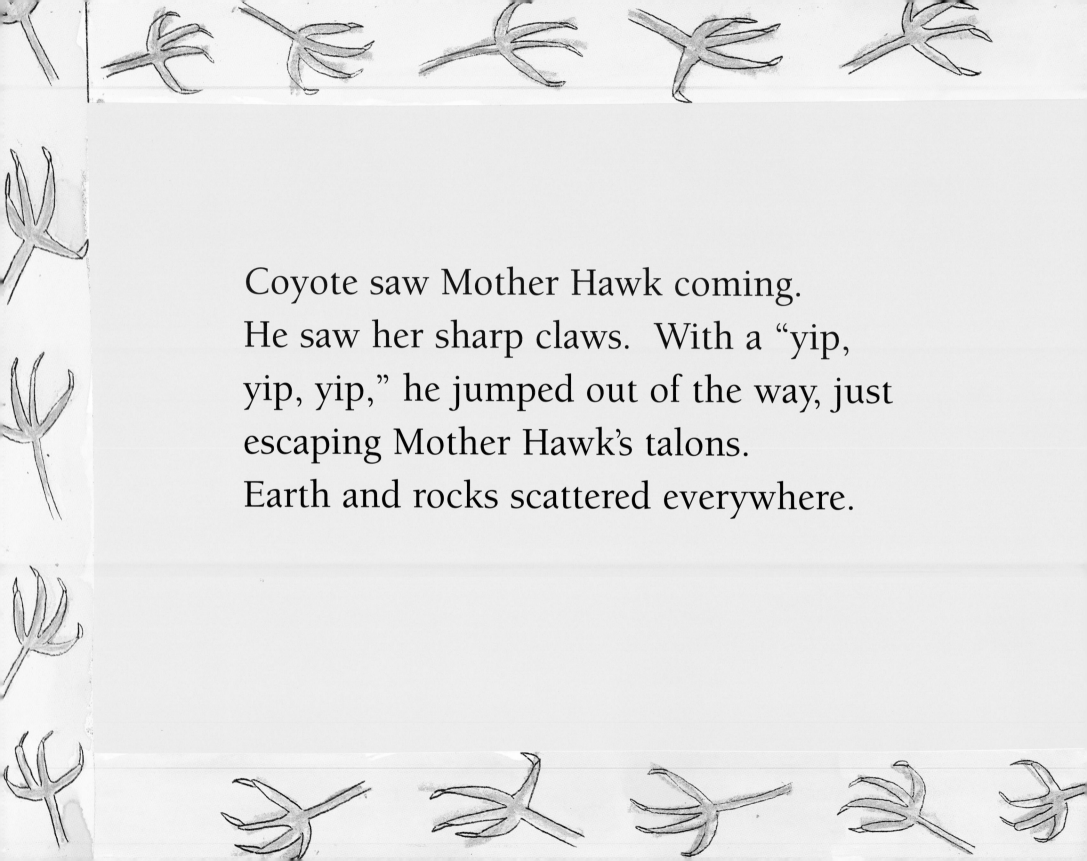

Coyote saw Mother Hawk coming.
He saw her sharp claws. With a "yip,
yip, yip," he jumped out of the way, just
escaping Mother Hawk's talons.
Earth and rocks scattered everywhere.

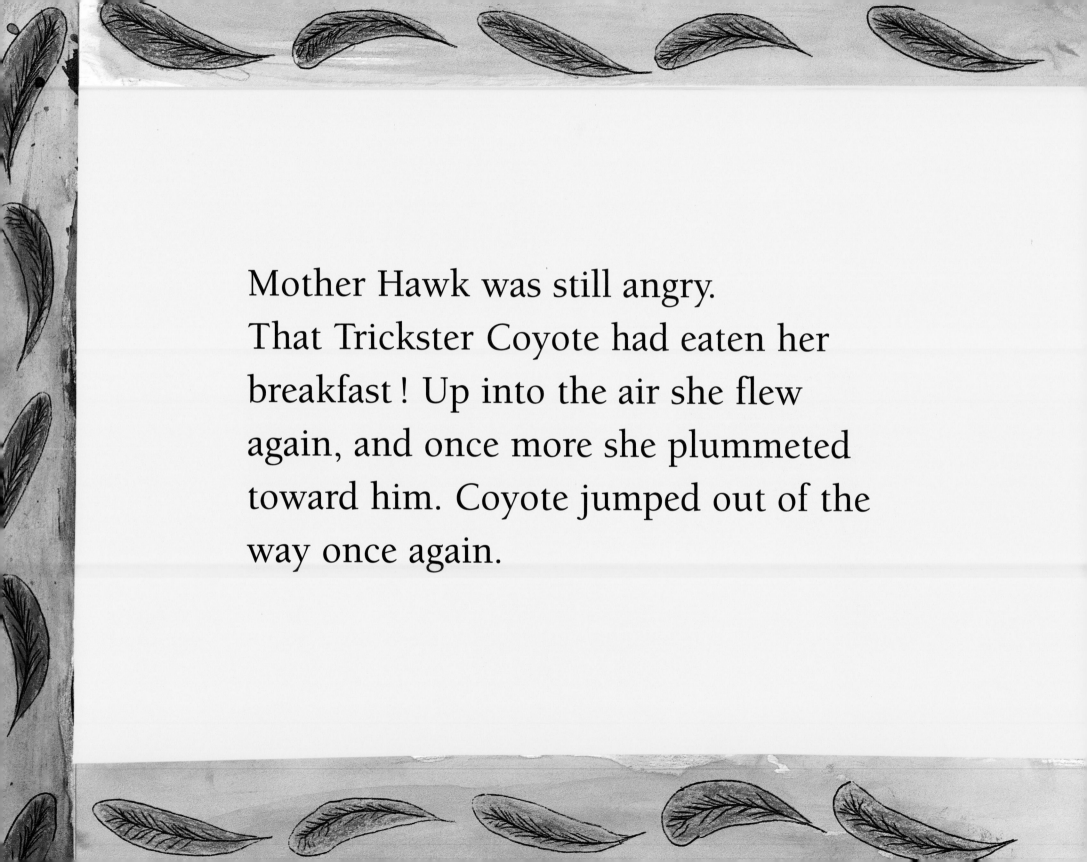

Mother Hawk was still angry.
That Trickster Coyote had eaten her
breakfast ! Up into the air she flew
again, and once more she plummeted
toward him. Coyote jumped out of the
way once again.

Mother Hawk let out a screech of rage.
Coyote knew he was in trouble.
Mother Hawk was mighty. She was
powerful. And she was trying to
catch him !

A third time Mother Hawk flew into the air. She was furious! With all the power she could gather, Mother Hawk circled in the air again. She plunged down at Coyote one last time.

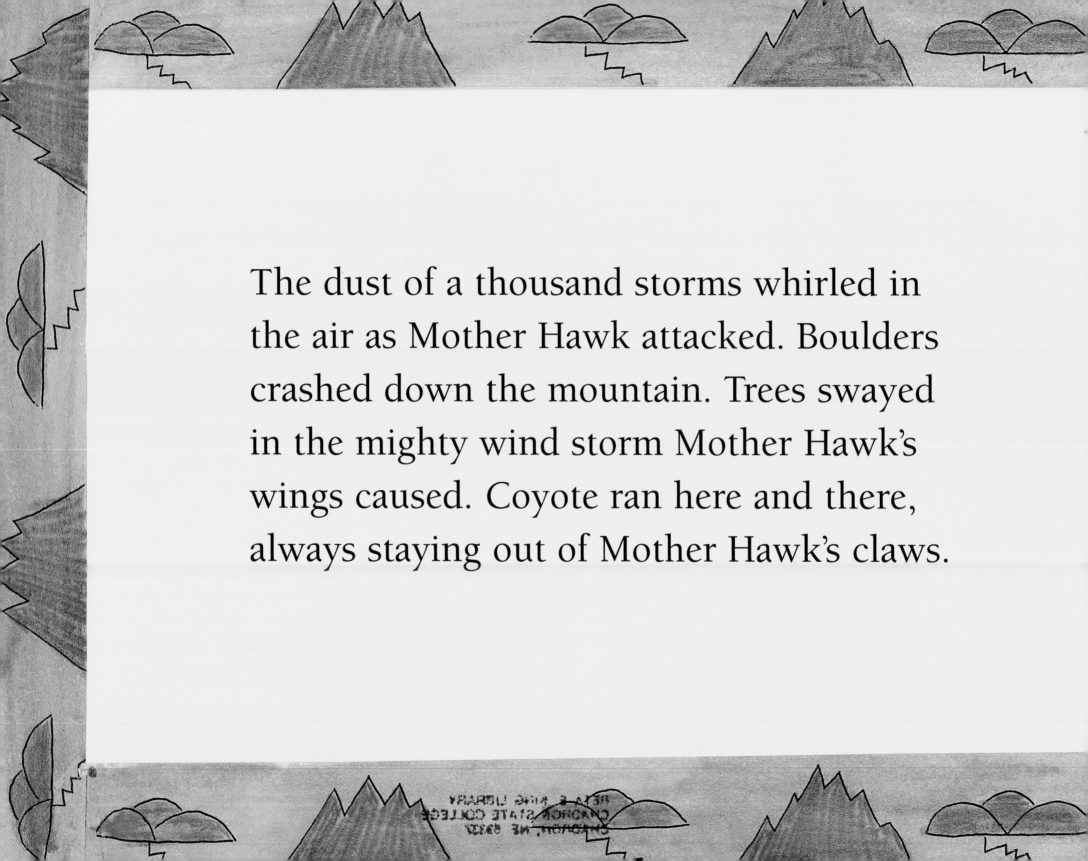

The dust of a thousand storms whirled in the air as Mother Hawk attacked. Boulders crashed down the mountain. Trees swayed in the mighty wind storm Mother Hawk's wings caused. Coyote ran here and there, always staying out of Mother Hawk's claws.

Mrs. Linares

At last Mother Hawk was no longer angry. As she landed in a tall tree to rest, the dust storm began to settle. And from that cloud rose a mountain greater than the rest. It was called Pia Toya.

The skyward peaks, scarred and jagged, bore the marks of Mother Hawk's claws. The cuts she made into the mountain started creeks and springs to trickle and flow with water.

Kristin Bishop

Coyote had seen Mother Hawk's anger.
He had seen her strength and power, and
he felt ashamed. Coyote disappeared in the
trees with his tail tucked between his legs.

Darby Linares

At last, the sun began to set, coloring the sky crimson. Mother Hawk flew high into the air. Below her, the new Deep Creek Range proved her power and might.

Marcie Thomas

ABOUT THE LEGEND

This retelling of *Pia Toya* is based on a traditional Goshute creation myth. Storytellers such as Maude Moon of the Goshute Indians are important and respected members of their tribes who remember and share the oral histories and tales of their people. The anecestral Goshutes gathered during winter months to hear these stories, which could not be told during the summer. It was considered dangerous to do so, perhaps because this was when the tribe was busy gathering food for the winter.

Hawks and coyotes play many of the main roles in Goshute mythology and the coyote, in particular, is a frequent figure in the legends and myths of other North American indigenous cultures. He represents many positive traits—spontaneity, playfulness, independence, and good humor, and the result of his exploits is often instructive. Yet Coyote's trickster nature can be very disruptive and cause much aggravation among his animal and human neighbors.

Pia Toya, which means big mountain, is pronounced *bee-ah DOY-ah*. *Isapai-ppeh*, Trickster Coyote, and *Kinnih-Pia*, Mother Hawk, are pronounced *EESH-ah-vipe* and *kee-nee-BEE-ah*.

Goshute storyteller Maude Moon.

ABOUT THE BOOK

The original manuscript from which *Pia Toya* was created began with a grant from the Utah State Office of Education. Book arts specialist Tamara Zollinger spent six months working with the talented and creative children and teachers at Ibapah Elementary School in 1995, teaching them the artistic techniques used to illustrate the project. The Bonneville Resource Conservation and Development Council, a nonprofit corporation which facilitates and seeks resources for projects of benefit to the people and communities of Utah, became interested in *Pia Toya* in 1998 and brought together the partnership of skilled and dedicated individuals as well as the generous sponsors needed to create the book you now hold.

ABOUT THE GOSHUTE PEOPLE

The name Goshute comes from the native word *Ku'tsip* or *Gu'tsip*, meaning people of ashes, desert, or dry earth. Most visitors to the Great Basin, the homeland of the Goshutes, find it a forbidding and harsh environment. In fact, the Great Basin is a high inland desert characterized by extreme aridity where all waters drain inward, having no outlet to the sea. But the Goshute ancestors knew this land and its resources well and were able to sustain themselves for centuries until the latter part of the nineteenth century when white pioneers began settling what had been an isolated part of the basin.

The Deep Creek Range, which Mother Hawk creates in the Pia Toya legend, is located in Utah's west desert near the state border with Nevada. It is among the most rugged of Utah's many mountain ranges and includes Ibapah Peak with an elevation of 12,087 feet. There are two Goshute reservations, home to the two distinct tribal bands residing in Utah : one, located in Skull Valley, is about ninety miles west of Salt Lake City ; the second and larger reservation, which is home to many of the children who illustrated this book, is about sixty miles south of Wendover, Nevada. This reservation, governed by the Confederated Tribes of the Goshute, is found at the base of the western slopes of the Deep Creek Range and encompasses about 525 square miles. It is home to a population of approximately 205 residents. Ibapah is a small rural community nearby. The town's name is an Anglicized form of the Goshute word *Ai-bim-pa*, meaning "white clay water," and refers to the waters of Deep Creek, which are laden with fine clay materials. Farming and ranching are the primary sources of revenue in the area.

Ibapah Peak, also known as Pia Toya, *is 12,087 feet high. Photograph courtesy of David F. Holz*

The Deep Creeks are abundantly vegetated with pine, juniper, aspen, and cottonwood trees. Other native plants include sagebrush, Indian paintbrush, Sego lilies, and elderberry. Rare bristlecone pines, some of which live to be thousands of years old, also grow along the craggy granite slopes.

Food   The ancestral Goshutes were sophisticated hunter-gatherers who used seeds, berries, roots, tubers, and greens from eighty-one species of vegetation. Pinyon pine nuts, one of the most important foods in the entire desert region, were gathered during the fall and stored for consumption during the winter months. Although most of the gathering was done by independent, self-sufficient family units, larger groups met for communal hunting several times each year. Rabbits, pronghorn antelopes, deer, mountain sheep, and under certain conditions waterfowl, fish, crickets, and grasshoppers, were all hunted cooperatively.

Way of Life   The Goshutes' nomadic way of life, dictated by the scarcity of water and the seasonal availability of food and other natural resources, meant that they had few material possessions ; they had no horses and carried what they needed from place to place. Tools and utensils were light and durable. Weaponry consisted mainly of bows made from cedar or other hardwood trees and strung with animal sinew. Arrowheads were made from obsidian, quartzite, limestone, and other hard minerals found in the Great Basin. Baskets, pots, grinding stones, flint knives and scrapers, and personal items such as ornaments constituted the balance of their belongings. If shelter was required, caves were used or simple windbreaks—small round bowers called wickiups—were constructed of available materials such as sagebrush. Clothing consisted of an apron, a basketry hat, and sometimes moccasins and a woven rabbitskin robe for warmth in winter.

The Goshutes have a long tradition of weaving willows to create baskets, cradleboards, and other items. Blankets were sometimes woven from branches of juniper and sage. Goshute women are still known for their weaving and for their expertise in working with deerskin, also known as buckskin, to make moccasins, gloves, necklaces, purses, belts, headbands, and bolo ties, all of which may be elaborately decorated with beadwork.

History   The first recorded contact between Goshutes and whites is found in the 1827 journal of trapper and mountain man Jedediah S. Smith. By 1846, the land that would become Utah was being crossed frequently by immigrants on their way to California. In 1847, followers of a then relatively new religion, The Church of Jesus Christ of Latter Days Saints, arrived to settle the valley of Great Salt Lake. The Mormons, as they are commonly known, began extending their settlements in all directions, and by the mid-1850s had begun farming and ranching enterprises in the desert west of the Salt Lake valley, bringing them into constant contact with the Goshutes. The establishment of the Overland Mail Company in 1858 and the Pony Express trail in 1860 brought increasing pressure to bear upon the previously isolated tribe.

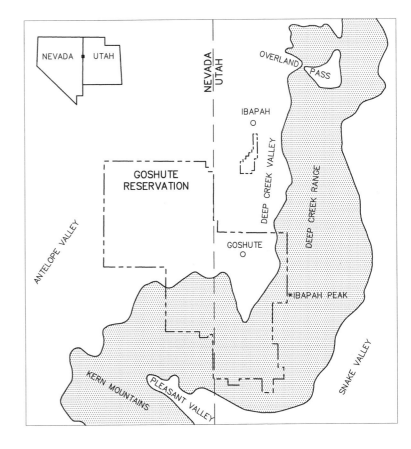

The reservation of the Confederated Tribes of the Goshute and its surroundings.

As was often the case when the expanding Western frontier brought whites and indigenous peoples together, conflict eventually erupted over the competition for natural resources. While the Goshutes had no concept of land ownership, the white settlers believed that unowned land and its resources were theirs to claim, settle, and cultivate. Hostilities between the two groups continued until October 12, 1863, when the Treaty of Tuilla was signed by U.S. government representatives and the designated Goshute tribal chiefs Tabby, Autosome, Tinta-pa-gin, and Harry-nap. While the treaty of "peace and friendship" called for the relocation of the Goshutes to reservations elsewhere in Utah and in the Oklahoma territory, the tribe continued living on its ancestral homelands. Some Goshute people participated in agricultural projects, establishing farms in the area with the aid and encouragement of the Mormons. Finally, in 1914, a permanent Goshute Indian Reservation was established near the Deep Creek Range.

Life Today   The Goshutes have retained much of their culture and many native religious ceremonies and practices. The tribal headquarters is the hub of tribal activities. Goshute youth are active in sports and are avid volleyball and softball players. Most children attend Ibapah Elementary School at Ibapah, Utah; older students commute daily to junior high and high schools some distance from the reservation.

In 1999, the Goshute youth expressed their pride in their ancestral heritage by requesting that a month be designated for learning about and honoring American Indian history. Utah Governor Michael Leavitt agreed with their petition, declaring November to be American Indian History Month and the twenty-second day of that month "Indigenous People's Day" in Utah.

ACKNOWLEDGMENTS

The Confederated Tribes of the Goshute, the Bonneville
Resource Conservation and Development Council, and the
University of Utah Press gratefully acknowledge the following
individuals and institutions for their generous support and
encouragement of this project :

Zeke and Katherine Dumke Jr.
Somers-Jaramillo and Company
Tooele County
U.S. Bank
Zions Bank/Simmons Family Foundation

This book would not exist without a grant from the Utah State
Office of Education ; the guidance of Tamara H. Zollinger ; the
dedication of Ibapah Elementary School teachers Marilyn
Linares (kindergarten through third grades) and John Thomas
(fourth through sixth grades) ; and, of course, the talent and
creativity of the children attending that school.

Borders painted by students
from kindergarten through
third grade classes :

Kristin Bishop
*
Kade Bateman
Megan Steele
*
Nora Bishop
Lamont Henroid
Remus Walema
*
Katie Tsinnie
Shanice Henroid

Illustrations created by
students from fourth through
sixth grade classes :

Rio Downs
Misty Yupe
Derrick Clover
Charmetria Walema
*
Nathan Hicks
Darby Linares
Klansey Bateman
Lorenzo Walema
Christina Clover
*
Marcie Thomas
Avery Walema

Special thanks to the Utah Division of Indian Affairs ; the
Goshute Tribal Council ; the Goshute Business Council ; Tribal
Chairman Milton Hooper ; Genevieve Fields, 1994 Tribal
Secretary ; Chrissandra Reed, 1994 Tribal Education
Coordinator ; Richard White, EarthFax ; Suzanne Somers ;
Ranae Bateman ; Carol Lynch Williams, and Holli D. Zollinger.

The children of Ibapah Elementary School and their teachers on
"Wear Red Day," October 1995.

Information concerning the Goshute Indian tribe was provided by the tribe as well as study and research conducted by several individuals : Dennis R. Defa ; Larry H. Godwin and Bruce D. Smith ; Jesse D. Jennings, Elmer R. Smith, and Charles E. Dibble ; Carling I. Malouf ; Nancy D. McCormick and John S. McCormick ; and Wick Miller.

Proceeds from the sale of this book benefit a cultural education foundation established in the name of the Confederated Tribes of the Goshute.

Tamara and Holli Zollinger